Appreciate
Each
Day

in 100+ Ways

Appreciate Each Day

in 100+ Ways

"Enjoy every moment
in life."

Janie Emerson

Cover Art by Georgeanna Lipe

ISBN: 978-0-9716320-1-1
Front cover watercolor by Georgianna Lipe
Book design by Janie Emerson
Printed in the United States of America.

JEM Enterprises
La Jolla, California

ShamrockWisdom.com

DEDICATED TO

Our heroes
and to all survivors
of violence.

May each of you
find lives of purpose,
hope, and peace.

INTRODUCTION

This book is for all ages. It is to inspire and open hearts to the wonders of the life around us. To appreciate the simplest thing and to see it all as special.

The left side of each page has been left blank. Make this book yours. Use it! Feel free to write your thoughts and draw your dreams.

Share this book with your whole family – adults, kids, seniors. Open to a page for all to appreciate for the day. Open to a page for quiet time at the end of the day.

This book is to calm, ground and quiet you. To let you appreciate the magic in the simple or the small.

To truly be able to –
Appreciate Each Day

100+ Ways
to
Appreciate
Each Day

This
is a day
of
joy and new
beginnings

Enjoy the
peace
of a
quiet
moment . . . . .

To
walk among
the
flowers —

I
feel the
rain
upon my
face....

The
hope & beauty
of
Each
Rainbow —

A
friend to
Lift
spirits in
our
need ....

This
day is
cold
&
chills
my
nose . . .

The
flight
of
geese poetends
snowfall . . . .

The
melodies of
happy
birds . . . .

The
warm peace
of a
cozy fire ....

The
smell of
cinnamon
on
frosty air —

Sunsets
so vibrant
~~they~~
~~are~~
alive —

Twinkling
stars
to
wish
upon . . . .

Today
I see
the
sparkle
of
frosty cold —

The
silvery
halo
of the
moon . . . .

The
majesty
of
sails before
the
wind —

Today
I see
blue
sky
&
cheer —

Rainbows
that
give beauty
to

our
sky . . . .

Today
I dance
in
fields
so
green —

The
chatter of
birds
greeting
a
new day —

This
day is
full
of.
dancing
daisys —

The
eternal
soothing
of
ocean waves . . .

To watch
the
painting
of
a
sunset . . . . .

To
see peace
in
the glow
of
the moon . . . .

To hear
the
wondrous
music
of
each day —

To
hear
silence
and
feel
renewed . . . .

Today
I feel
the
warm rays
of the
sun —

The
fragile scent
of
emerging
Spring.....

The
soft love
in a
child's
eyes....

The
happiness
of
sunshine
on
my
face —

Today
I watch
hummingbirds
hover to
feed —

Today
I smell
salty
sea air.....

A
candle
illumines
with
a
golden
glow —

Today
I watch
the
river flow
on
&
on . . . .

Today
I
appreciate
the
~~freedom~~
to
be —

To
see life
in
flowers
unfold . . . .

Today
I smell
the
wake of
Spring —

To
see love
is
the eyes
of a
friend . . . . .

Today
I watch
the
chase of
clouds
on
high.....

To
feel the
joy
of
giving —

This day
is
warm
with golden
sun . . . .

Today
I see the
view
~~from~~
mountaintop —

To
see the glee
in a
wagging
tail —

Today
I smell
a
sweet, red
Rose . . . .

I
embrace Spring
and
it's new
life . . . . .

A
day of
sunshine,
Love,
&
~~butterflies~~ . . . .

Today
I appreciate
all the
friends
I
have —

A
small hand
of
trust
in
mine . . . . .

Today
I watch
nests
made up
of
twigs —

The
contented
rumble
of a
kitty's
purr . . . .

The
unspoken
truth
of
souls
as
one . . . .

Today
I
celebrate
a
healthy
me —

The
joy of
gifts
eagerly
Received . . . . .

Today
I feel
the
spray of
Rain . . . .

A
puppy's yelps
of
~~great~~
glee —

The
glitter of dewdrops
on a
special rose . . . .

The
freedom of
summer embraces
all
outdoors —

Today,
I appreciate
the
Rolling
sea —

The
gentle whisper
of the
forest —

The
soft rustle
of
green grass . . . . .

This
day is
filled
with birds
at
song —

Today
I watch
the
fluffy, white
clouds . . . .

The
freedom of
riding
upon the
air —

Today
I see a baby
bird's
1st
flight —

A
gentle breeze
~~that~~
caresses
my
face....

The
joyful babble
of
water
in a
brook . . . .

The
cooling shelter
of the
TREES —

A
gentle Rain
bathes
all in
diamonds
of
delight....

This
day is
clear,
&
crisp,
&
blue . . . .

The
nip of salty
air
on
nose & cheeks —

The
iridescent
glow of
hummingbirds
in
flight ....

Fireflies
twinkling
lights
of
joy —

Today
I see the
glow
of
setting sun —

Joyous
Laughter
that
lightens
my
world . . . .

Today,
I appreciate
all
of me —

Today
I watch
the
Rolling waves....

I
watch
Dolphins
joyfully at
play —

Today
I watch
the
promise
of
spring
unfold . . . .

The
eager licks
of
puppy
love —

To
hear children's
Laughter
at
play —

Today
I appreciate
all in
my
life . . . .

A
song
that creates
sunshine
in
my heart —

This
day is
filled
with
happy
sounds —

To
see the joy
in
the eyes
of
a child —

Today
I
walk through
trees
so
grand . . . .

Today
I crunch
through
Leaves
of
gold . . . .

Fall's
joyous colors
paint
the TREES —

The.
Rush of joy —
embrace t
it
all . . . .

Today
I stand atop
a
grassy
hill . . . .

Today
I see myself
and
love
"my me" . . . .

A
waem hug
to lift
the
heaet —

A
smile upon
a
~~baby's face~~ . . . .

The
happy purring
of a
furry friend —

The
sunrise
bathes all
in
new life —

I
feel winter
in
contrasts
of
cold & warm....

The
pure silence
of
first snow....

The
excitement of
a
New Year's
Eve! ___

The
total
knowing
of
true
friends —

To
have the
joy
of
Receiving
love —

Holding
hands
to
connect
the
hearts . . . . .

Today
I appreciate
ALL
I see . . . .

ABOUT THE AUTHOR

JANIE EMERSON

Janie Emerson is the author of the successful *The Magic of Me, Guided By Animal Angels*, and *Walking With Angels*. Her writings appear in newspapers and magazines. She has won national awards for her poetry and is a respected consultant and acclaimed speaker.

The inspiration for her writings comes from life. Janie's work gives balance, insight and focus to life's events. Her intent is to empower and to enhance your life.

Janie lives in La Jolla, California with her husband Bob and her beloved Westies. She has been an advocate for women owned businesses nationally and an active community leader. Janie is currently working on two great new projects.

ShamrockWisdom.com

www.ingramcontent.com/pod-product-compliance
Lightning Source LLC
Chambersburg PA
CBHW062057290426
44110CB00022B/2628